The Tucson Artifacts

An Album of Photography
with Transcriptions and Translations
of the Medieval Latin

Donald N. Yates

Photography by Robert C. Hyde

Longmont: Panther's Lodge
2017

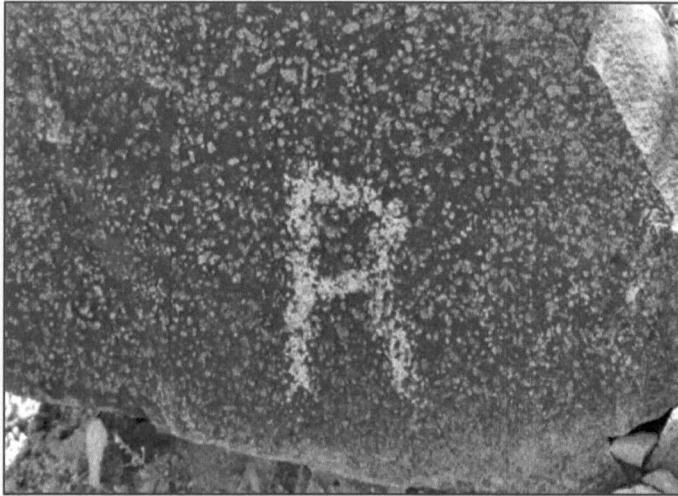

Pecked petroglyph R in Roman square capital script on Signal Hill guarding the approach to the Silverbell site (cover) matches that of ninth-century Tucson Artifacts, where it stands for "Romans."

ISBN 13: 978-0692727089
ISBN 10: 0692727086

Second corrected edition: Jan. 2017

Preface

Now that nearly a century has passed since the so-called Tucson Crosses or Silverbell Artifacts were excavated in the compacted soil of the Santa Cruz river valley outside Tucson, Arizona in the years between 1924 and 1930, it seems appropriate to tell the fuller story of their meaning for Southwest archeology and indeed world history. There are thirty-five cast lead artifacts, counting double crosses as two and pieces of swords or spears that join to form one. Only one is not lead, the Theodore memorial from native caliche that constitutes artifact no. 2.

All form part of the 1994 bequest to the Arizona Historical Society Museum, Southern Division by Thomas W. Bent, Jr., where they are split between display cases in the lobby and the vault.

The crosses and related objects, including two nehushtans, were made by the lost-wax process from lead, a favored medium for lasting memorials in antiquity and valuable by-product from the gold-silver-and-copper mining carried on by various foreign visitors in Arizona. They are covered with medieval Latin and square Hebrew inscriptions that provide a record of a military colony of Frankish and Breton Jews who conquered the Toltec fortress city of Rhoda we now know as Tumamoc Hill overlooking Tucson, an ancient and important trading and mining site among the Hohokam Indians. The founders called their new realm Calalus ("Wasteland" in Hebrew) and it lasted from 780 until 900, when it was destroyed by earthquakes, and the king returned with a large part of his followers to Mexico. At this crossroads of civilizations in ninth century West Mexico we also detect Chinese seal script, Hindu cult objects, Mesoamerican glyphs, images of Jewish and Christian temples, Celtic ogam inscriptions and what might be called "pre-Templar" symbols.

On March 11-14, 2015, with the assistance of Laraine Daly Jones and Doreen Crowe, we were able to take formal studio shots of the entire accession catalogued as 94.26.1AB-32. A record of that photo session is compiled in this publication with the hope that such a collection of plates paired with matching inventory notes will aide us in preparation of a scholarly monograph on the Tucson Artifacts, as well as be of possible use to the owner institution, people of Arizona and public at large.

Donald N. Yates
January 1, 2017

1A. The Great Cross

Catalog #94.26.1A. s. IX^{ex}. Larger half of cast lead joined double Latin cross with gold infill inscriptions. Discovered September 13, 1924 by Charles E. Manier. 45-46 cm tall, 30 cm wide, 3.2 cm thick. Letters about 1 cm high. 43 lbs. 1 oz.

In memo(r)iam/ Romani/ Aetius/ Britannia Gaul/5 Albion   Seine/ Theodorus/ Iacobus Israel,/ consu(l)es urbium/ magnarum com/10 septi(nge)nti mil-/ itibus. A.D. DCCC/ Kal(endas) Ian(uarias).

To the memory of Romans: Britain and Albion's Jacob, to that second Aëtius, Theodore, and to Israel of the Seine Province in Gaul, consuls of mighty cities with seven hundred soldiers each. A.D. 800, January 1. We are transports on the sea. Calalus is Terra Incognita. The Toltec governor was as a king ruling widely o'er the peoples. They were transferred, Theodore deploying his troops before the city of Rhoda, and more than seven hundred captives were taken. Not one of them in the city was exempted from gold. Theodore, a true man of the highest valor, reigns for fourteen years. Jacob reigns for six, God aiding him. Have no fear. In the name of (the God of) Israel. Oliver.

1-7 *These lines are arranged and grouped around the three busts with the names* Iacobus, Theodorus *and* Israel. *3* Aetius *misread by Covey* Actius. *The allusion is to the Roman general Flavius Aëtius (d. 454), "the last of the Romans." 5* Seine *official alternate historical Medieval Latin spelling for the name of the river and province centered on Paris, the Merovingian capital;* Sequona *is the classical form. See* Gallia Judaica, *p. 650. 9* com *sic pro* cum. *10 hyphen appears in the original where the missing letters have been supplied; perhaps* septienti *was intended. 12 The Romans and particularly the Papacy started the New Year at Christmas (Saturnalia). The date January 1, 800 corresponds to the week following the coronation of Charlemagne as the first Holy Roman Emperor in Rome.*

7

Prouehimur pelago. Calalus terra incogn-/
ita. Populum late regem Toltezus/ Siluanus.
Traducti sunt, Theodorus/ suas copias
subucie urbe Rhoda et plus/5 septin-gentia
capti. Nullus auro/ urbe eximentur.
Theod<o>rus uir sum-/mae uirtutis regnat
inter annos/ quattuordecim. Iacobus regnat
inter sex,/ Deo adiuuante. Non
timendum. /10 In nomine − Israel.
Ol(iuerus).

---

1 Prouehimur *etc. cf. 4, 18-2. Probably part of a
military anthem like the trochaic septenarii of
Roman soldiers and medieval church
processionals.* Calalus *indeclinable foreign word;
cf. Hebrew* khalal חלל *'empty, waste, used up.'*
4 subucie *perhaps instead of* subuice. *Covey
reads* subcie *and translates "to
the foot of the city."* Rhoda *Greek 'rose-tree, rose
of Sharon, Red Isle, Red City'; cf. Hopi, Zuni*
Palatkwapi, *Nahuatl* Chichilticalli *'Great Red
City of the South.'* 2 Toltezus *indeclinable
foreign word (also used in 5A line 16), Toltec,
Ancient Mexican, urban dweller, tradesman,
craftsman; cf. Nahuatl* Tōltēcatl. populum late
regem *has perhaps the sense of 'regional ruler,'
as in Aeneid I 21; cf.* Theodoricus, *Gothic*
Theuderic *'ruler of the peoples.'* 3 Siluanus *cf.
Pima* si'wan *'governor, chief, priest.'* 5-6 *Covey
reads, "No gold is taken away." The meaning
seems to be rather that not a single of the captives
taken by the Romans was exempted from
providing gold tribute to the Toltec governor
(*Toltezus Silvanus*), whom Theodore replaced.*
6 Theodrus *cf.* Todros *(Hebrew and Byzantine
form of the name).* 7 inter *cf. French* entre,
Spanish entre, *'for the course of.'* 10 OL *is an
official's siglum, or diplomatic mark, with the
lower stroke of the L exaggerated and drawn out
to indicate the rest of the name, which appears to
be* Oliverus; *cf. the OF name* Olieu.

1B. The Great Cross

Catalog #94.26.1B. s. IX[ex]. Smaller of joined cast lead Latin crosses with gold infill inscriptions. Discovered September 13, 1924 by Charles E. Manier. 45-46 cm tall, 30 cm wide, 1.3 cm thick. Lettering 0.5 to 1.2 cm. 19 lbs. 15 oz.

Urre renatus
Iacobus/ Deo
iuuante regnat Iacobus/
manu forti more
maiorum./ Cantatur
Domino. Fama semper
uiuat./
[5] Ol(iuerus).

1 Urre *gold, mine, treasure; cf. OF* urhe, *Basque* urre, *Old Spanish* urro, *Spanish* oro. *Covey corrects to* urbe *and translates,* "Jacob renews the city." 4 Cantatur Domino *cf. Psalms 67:5, 95:1-2, 97:1.* Fama semper uiuat *cf. Psalms 110:10, 113B:18.*

Reborn with gold was Jacob. With God helping him, he reigned with a strong hand in the way of his ancestors. Sing unto the Lord. May his fame live forever. Oliver.

11

2. The Theodore Memorial
Catalog #94.26.2. Dated 800. Flat, roughly equilateral-triangle-shaped slab of caliche with epitaph. Discovered September 14, 1924 by Charles E. Manier and Karl Ruppert. 31 x 28 x 30 cm, 6 cm thick. 7 lbs. 1 oz.

 Iacob[us] Theodor[us]
  A.D. DC[C]C (?)

Jacob   Theodore.
Anno Domini 800. (?)

3A. The Ab Ovo Cross

Catalog #94.26.3A. s. IX[ex]. First half of double joined cast lead Latin cross with gold infill inscriptions. Discovered November 28, 1924 by Thomas W. Bent, Sr. 28.5 cm tall, 21.75 cm wide, 1.5 cm thick. Letters about 1 cm high. 7 lbs. 8 oz.

Ab ouo./ A.D. DCCXL./ A.D. DCCCC./ Nil nisi cruce. Flagrante bello obiit Israel./5 Orate pro anima Israel. Sicut patribus/ sit Deus nobis. Sit tibi terra leuis. Decori/ decus addit auito. Israel fidei defensor./ Israel sept-/ em et sexa-/10 ginta reg-/nat annos./

Israel secundus regnat inter/ sex. Israel septimus sex et/ uiginti annos natus regnare/ coepit. Bellum internelinum [sic]./ 15 Aut uincere aut mori. Auito/ uiret honore de die in diem.

---

5 Sicut patribus *cf. I Kings 8:57.* 8-9 *Covey emends* Septimus (VII) *to* Tertius (III). 14 *Should be* internecinum.

From the beginning, A.D. 790-900. Naught but by the cross. While war raged, Israel died. Pray for the soul of one of Israel. As unto our fathers, so may God be unto us. May the earth lie lightly upon thee. He adds honor to that of our forefathers. Israel was a defender of the faith. He reigned sixty-seven years.

Israel the Second reigns for six years. Israel VII has now begun his reign at twenty-six years old. It has been a war to the death. To vanquish or die. Flourishing with ancestral honor, day after day.

15

3B. The Ab Ovo Cross

Catalog #94.26.3B. s. IX^{ex}. Second half of 3A. Discovered November 28, 1924 by Thomas W. Bent, Sr. 28.5 cm tall, 21.75 cm wide, 1.5 cm thick. Letters about 1 cm high. 4 lbs. 8 oz.

Ad utrumpue at spes non fracta/ die [sic] gratia. Elapso tempore ex/ aduerso fons et origo malorum/ uenit summa dies et/[5] ineluctabile tempus./ Adsum Dominus uobiscum./ Ol[iuerus].

---

1 at *is an abbreviation for* autem. 2 *Should be* deo gratia ("thanks be to God"). *Covey suggests possibly* die gratiae ("in our day of grace"). 3 *Covey says it should read* origine. 6 In die illa: Quia ego ipse qui loquebar, ecce adsum (Is. 52:6). 4-5 *Vergil, Aeneid II 324.*

In either event, however, our hope will not be crushed, thanks be to God. With time slipping by, on the other hand, that font and source of evil, now comes our last day and the unavoidable end. I the Lord am with ye. Oliver.

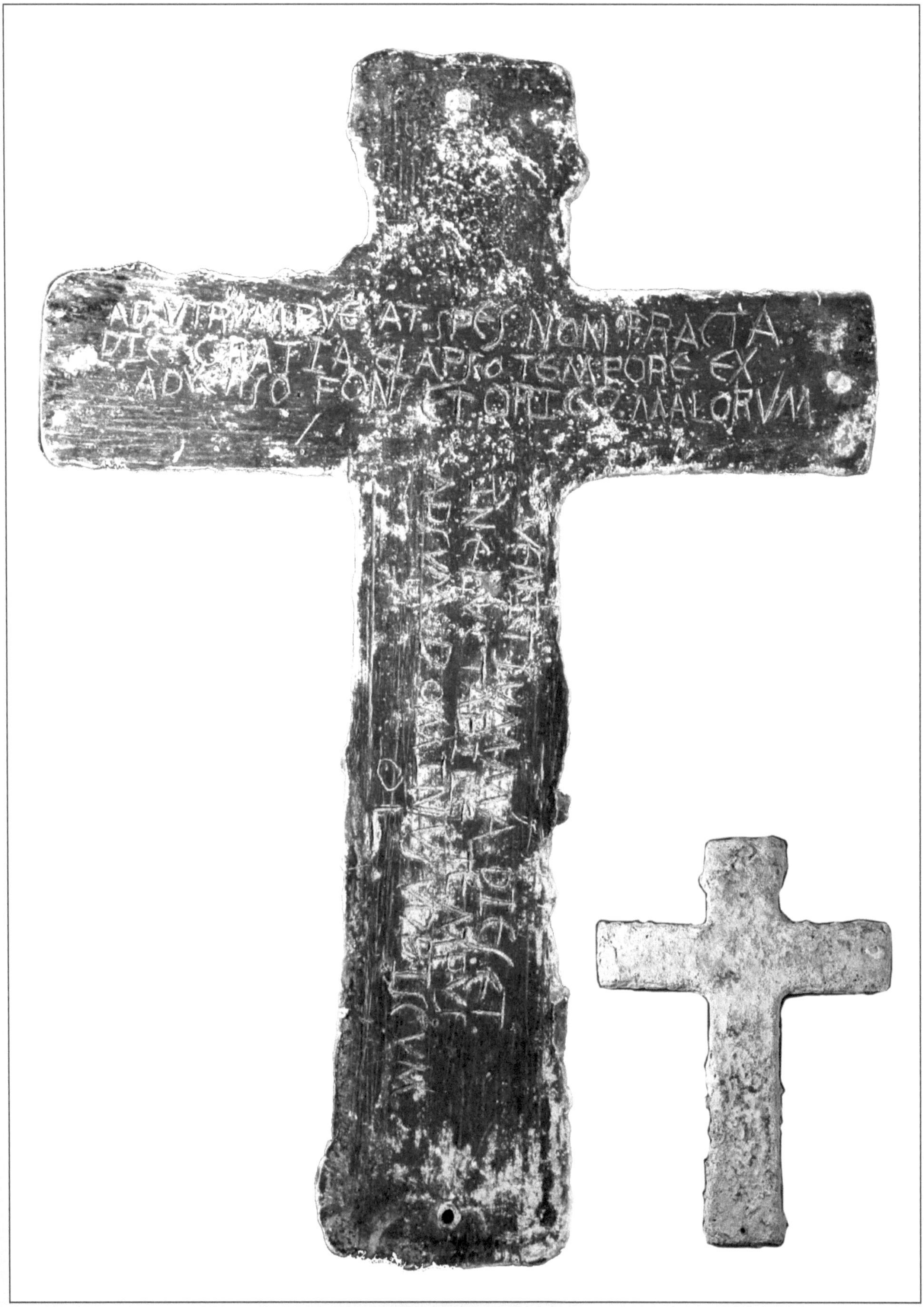

4. The Albion Cross

Catalog #94.26.4. s. IX^{ex}. Discovered November 30, 1924 by Charles E. Manier. Single cast lead Latin cross with gold infill lettering. 29.5 cm tall, 20.75 cm wide, 0.5 to 3.5 cm thick. Letters 0.6 to 0.8 cm high. 5 lbs. 8 oz.

L[euitae]
✝ Albion
Theodorus
Iacobus

Romani
prouehimur

To the memory of Levites: Theodorus and his successor Iacobus of Albion. We are Roman transports.

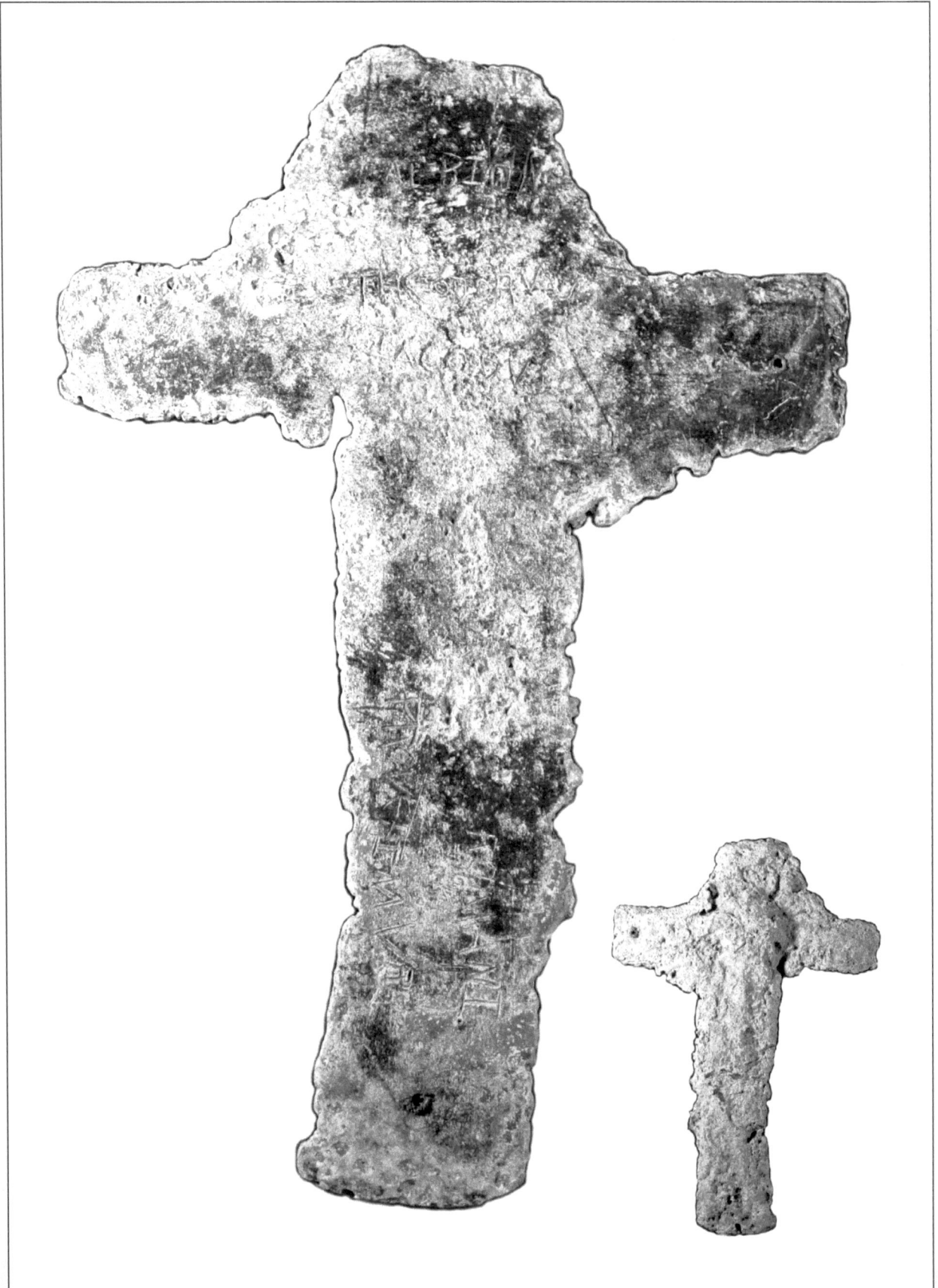

5A. The Josephus Cross

Catalog #94.26.5A. s. IX[ex]. Cast lead double Latin cross with gold infill lettering. Discovered December 5, 1924 by Charles E. Manier and Thomas W. Bent, Sr. 28.5 cm tall, 21.75 cm wide, 1.5 cm thick. Letters about 1 cm high. 5 lbs. 5 oz.

Regnauit/ populorum/ Beniaminus./ Ab Seine Roma-/[5] m uenerunt/ Gallorum for-/ tissimi. Venit populi auxilio urbi funda-/ menta iacere. Murum urbi circumdedit/ hostibus resistere. Ingens uirium Ben-/[10] iaminus. Multitudinem religionis impl-/ euit. Occisus est a Theban[i]s. Hoc audiui de/ parenti meo annis quingentis/ post post montem [sic]. In memoriam patris. Iosephus.

[15] A.D. DCCCLXXX. Isreal [sic] tertius/ cum Toltezus liberasset expulsus/ est. Primus morem soluit. Terra/ tremit. Mortalia corda stra-/ uit pauor. Anno tertio pos-/[20] tquam profugerat se in urbe/ receperunt [?] murisque se tene-/ bant. Hominem mortuum ne [?]/ urbe ne [continues on Cross 5B] . . .

---

11 Thebaiis *might have been the original text. Thebani could refer either to a type of foot soldier armed with a lance or pike (not necessarily one from Thebes), or to Gothic warriors, or, as a projection backward in history, to the Byzantines whose armies were often drawn from northern Greece. The Aurelian Walls, still partly standing today, were built to protect Rome from a feared Gothic attack beginning 270. In the second half of the third century, mixed Gothic armies and navies ravaged the Aegean world, including Thebes and Athens itself. Contemporaries weren't sure how to identify them but referred to them by various names, often as "Thracians." They were reduced, some being resettled in the Balkans by the emperor Claudius Gothicus and his successor Aurelian. The "Aurelian" walls were continually repaired and augmented in the late 3rd through late 5th century, notably under Honorius 395-425. Nevertheless, Rome was sacked by the Visigoths in 410, Vandals in 455 and Ostrogoths in 546. The Aurelian Walls still stood strong when Rome was attacked by the Byzantine and Lombard armies in the 8th century.* 22-23 ne urbe *should be* in urbe.

Benjamin was ruler o'er the peoples. It is from the Province of the Seine to Rome that the bravest of the Gauls have always come. So Benjamin came to the aid of the people to lay the foundation for the City. He built a perimeter wall for the City. Of enormous strength was Benjamin. He filled the multitudes with awe. He was killed by Thebans. This I heard from my father five hundred years afterwards after his death. In memory of my father. Josephus.

Anno Domini 880. Israel III, for freeing the Toltecas, was exiled. He was the first to break with the custom. There was an earthquake. Panic laid low all mortal hearts. The third year after he had fled abroad, they returned to the city and kept within the walls. A dead man *[continues on Cross 5B]* . . .

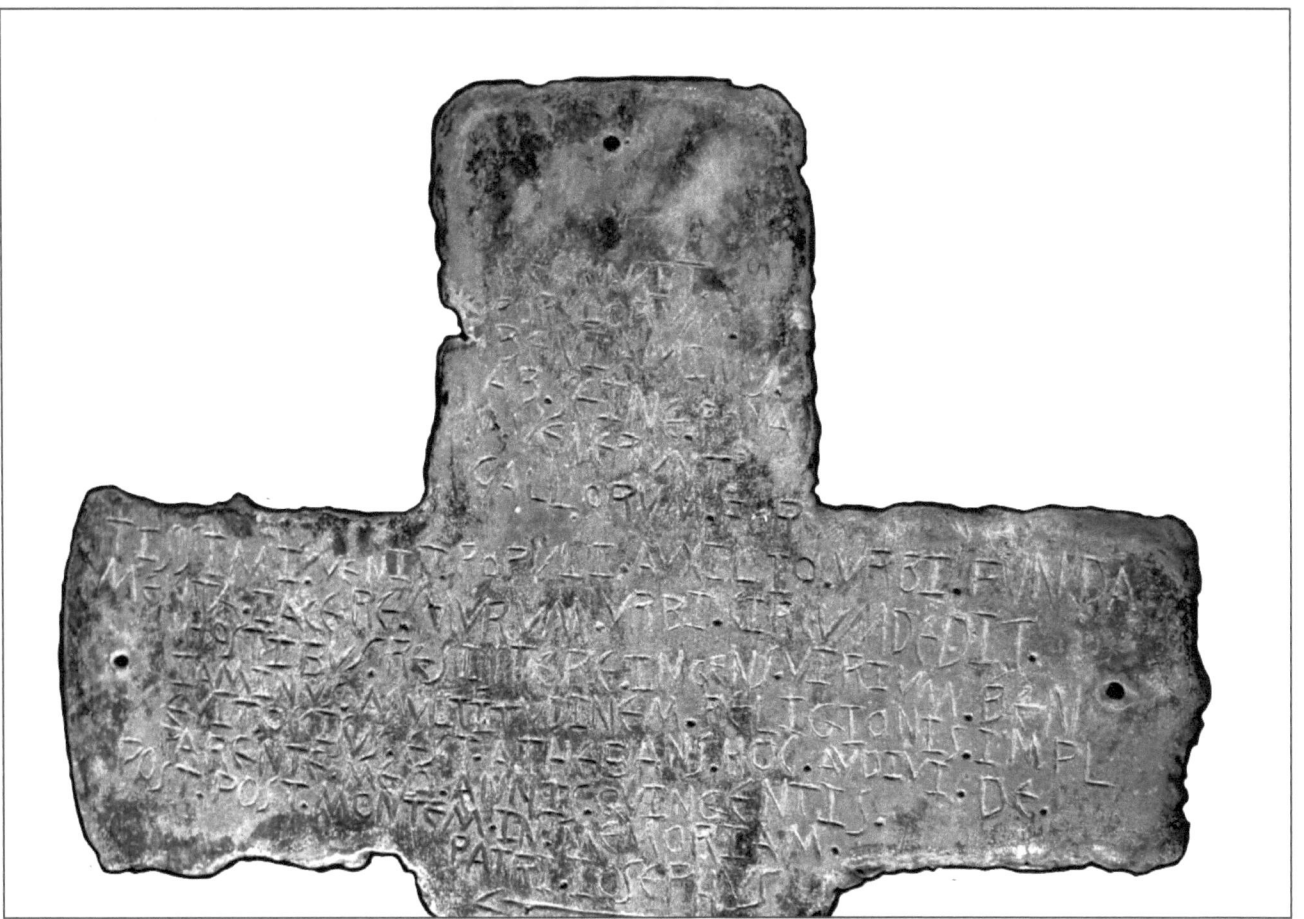

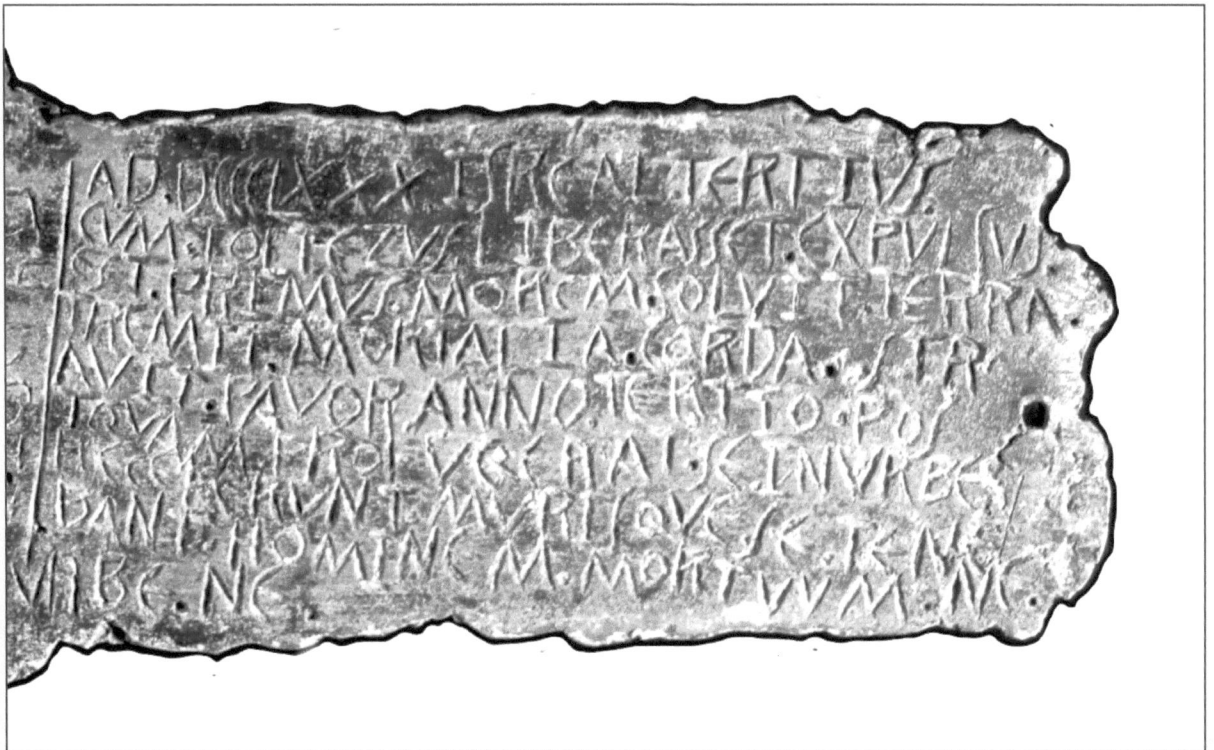

5B. The Josephus Cross

Catalog #94.26.5B. s. IX[ex]. Second of cast lead joined twin crosses with gold infill lettering. Discovered December 5, 1924 by Charles E. Manier and Thomas W. Bent, Sr. 28.5 cm tall, 21.75 cm wide, 1.5 cm thick. Letters about 1 cm high. 4 lbs. 2 oz.

sepelito neue/ urito. Ante/ urbe[m] planities/ patebat. Colles/ [5] urbe[m] cingeban-/ t. Centum an-/ ni sunc [sic] cum/ rex fuit Iacobus. Iacobus/ in prima acie uersari. Omnia proui-/[10] dere. Mult[itudin]em ipse pugnare./ Saepe hostem ferire. Israel/ sacerdotibus creandis animum/ adiecit. Nobis uita est populis late/ regem. Ol[iuerus].

[15] A.D. DCCCXCV. Terra incogni[t]a. Utina-/m conata efficere possim regi/ seruire. Incertum est quam/ longa uita futura sit. Mul-/ ta sunt quae dici possunt flagra-/[20] nti bello. Caesi sunt tria milia./ Dux cum principibus capiuntur./ Nihil aliud nisi pax quaesita/ est. Deus omnia constituit./ Ol[iuerus].

———————————————

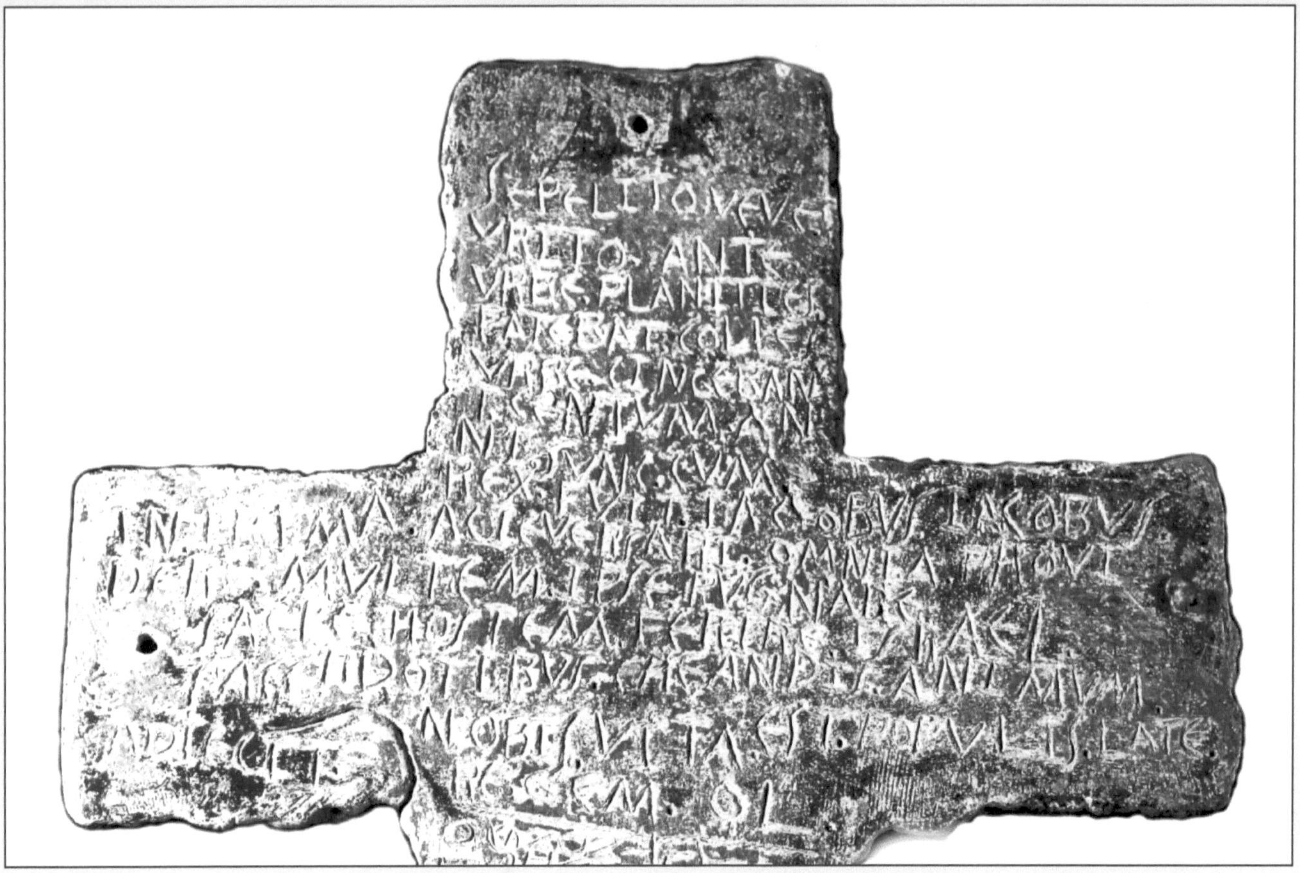

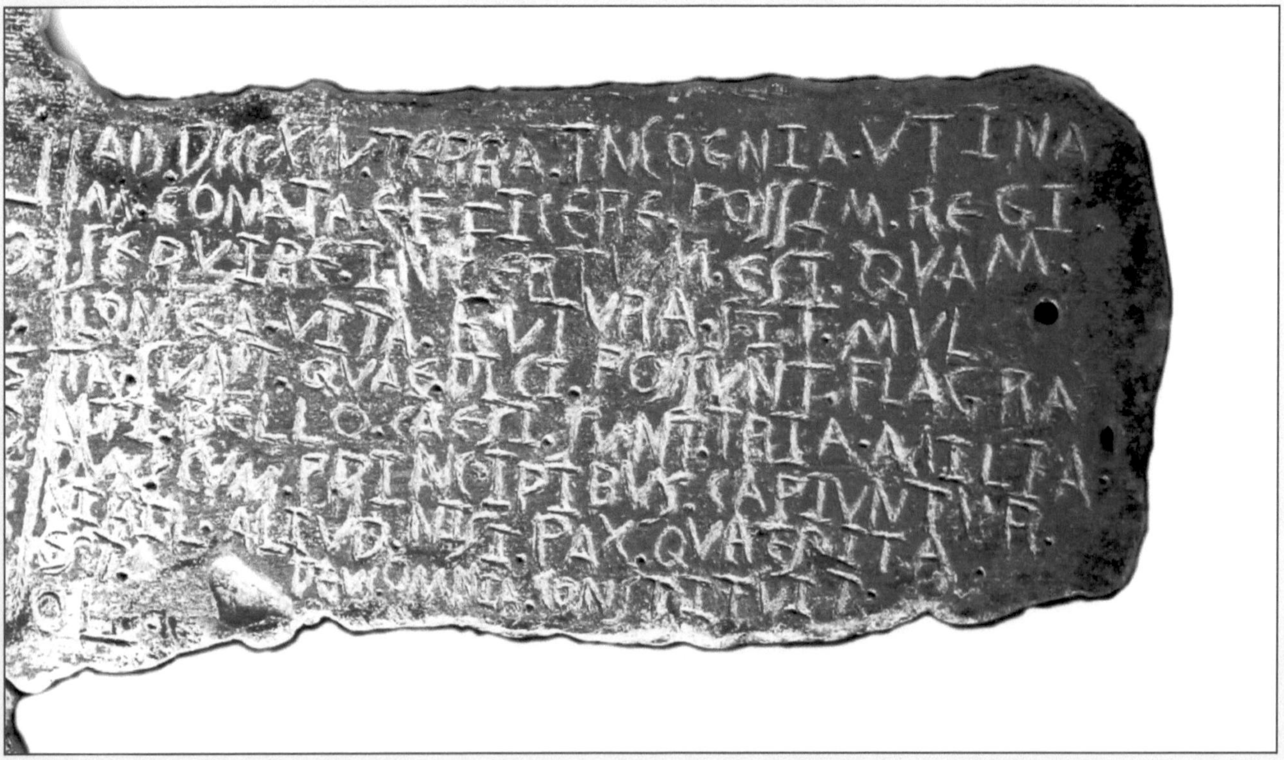

. . . thou shalt neither bury nor burn within the city. Before the city lay a plain. Hills ringed it round. It has been one hundred years since Jacobus was king. Jacobus would throw himself into the thick of battle. He saw to everything. He would fight a multitude of men by himself. Often did he smite the foe. Israel turned his attention to creating priests. Ours is rather a life of rulers of men.

Anno Domini 895. Terra Incognita. Would that I could finish my efforts to serve the king. It is uncertain how long this way of life will continue. Many things could be said with this war raging. Three thousand have been slaughtered. The leader with all his principal followers has been taken captive. We sought nothing but peace. But God ordains all things. Oliver.

6A. The Judas-Benjamin-Isaac Cross

Catalog #94.26.6A. s. IX[ex]. Slender double Latin cross with pictograms, diagrams, seals, mottoes and names. Discovered January 24, 1925 by Karl Ruppert. 39 cm tall, 22 cm wide, 1.5 cm thick. Letters about 1 cm high. 5 lbs. 6 oz.

S[acrum].
L[euitae]. I[sraelitae].
Iudas
Beniaminus
Isaacus
V-O-E
In memo[r]iam

---

6 VOE Vincit omnia exercitia (?) *practice and continuous exercise (exercitia) by skilled soldiers in daily training results in victory (victoria)" – Hrabanus Maurus, De procinctu romanae miliciae, praef., ch. 1.; cf. Bachrach, p. 129, Vegetius, De re militare III 2.*

Sacred
Levites and Israelites
Judas
Benjamin
Isaac
Practice Conquers All
Oliver

6B. The Judas-Benjamin-Isaac Cross

Catalog #94.26.6B. s. IX^{ex}. Second of slender joined cast lead crosses. Discovered January 24, 1925 by Karl Ruppert. 39 cm tall, 22 cm wide, 1.5 cm thick. Letters about 1 cm high. 4 lbs. 13 oz.

R[oma].
T.O.B.
[. . .]
Beniaminus laudatur

We are of Rome. (Our temple commemorates) the Good Name (of King David). Benjamin is praised.

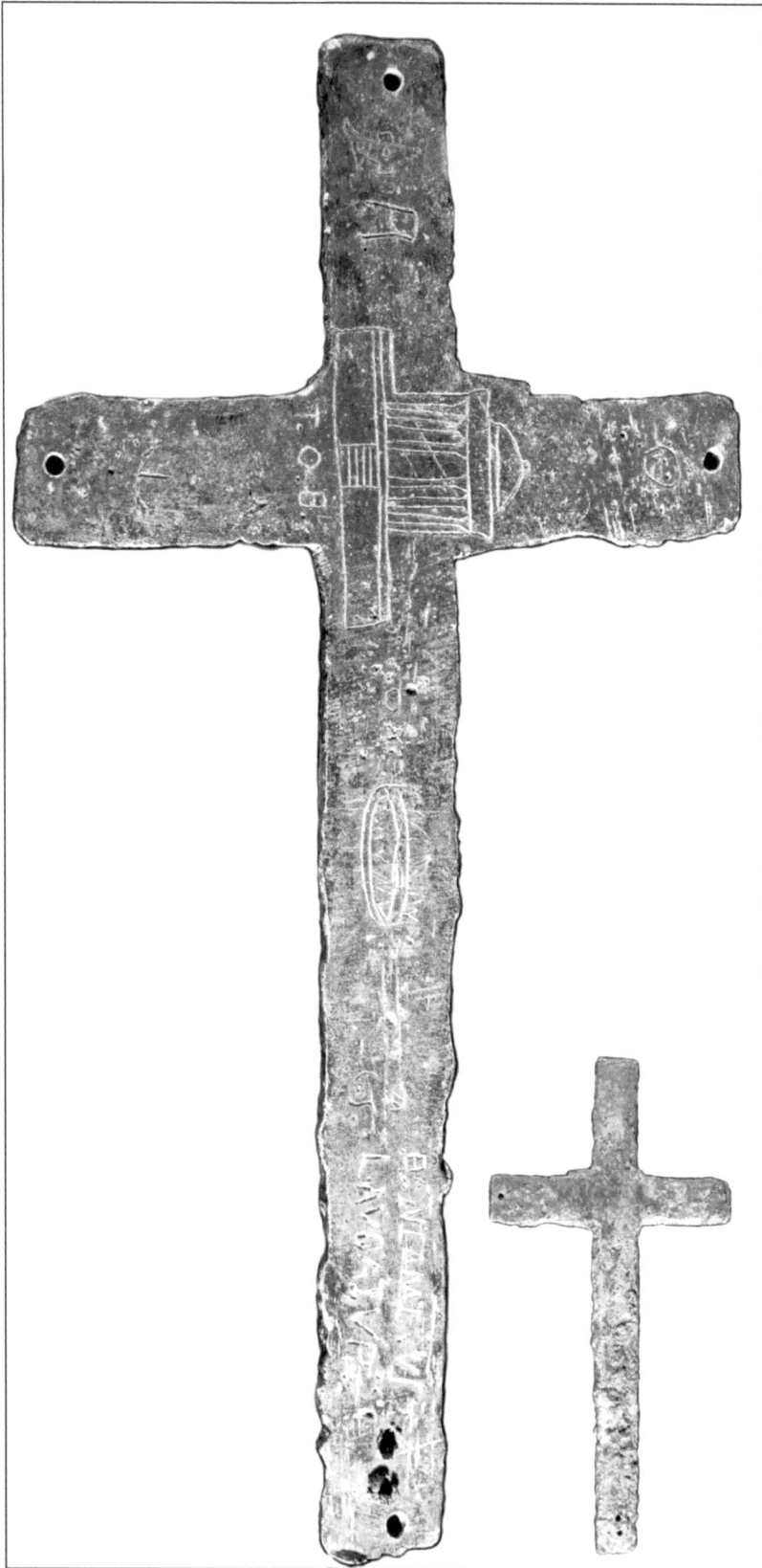

31

7A. The Josephus and Saul Cross

Catalog #94.26.7A. s. IX^{ex}. Double cast lead riveted cross with gold infill markings. Discovered January 24, 1925 by Karl Ruppert. 31 cm tall, 19 cm wide, 1.5 cm thick. Letters about 1 cm high. 3 lbs. 1 oz.

L[euitae].
Iosephus
Saulus
In memo[r]iam

spice spoon, trident, seal, mitres

Levites. To the memory of Josephus and Saul

7B. The Josephus and Saul Cross

Catalog #94.26.7B. s. IX^{ex}. Second of cast lead crosses riveted together. Discovered January 24, 1925 by Karl Ruppert. 31 cm tall, 19 cm wide, 1.5 cm thick. Letters about 1 cm high. 3 lbs. 5 oz.

R[omani].
Iosephus laudatur

A Roman. Joseph is praised.

Seals, ship

Frankish axe

8. Short Sword Catalog #94.26.8. s. IX. Cast lead practice or ceremonial short sword (*gladius*). Discovered February 13, 1925 by Charles E. Manier. 44.5 cm long (33.6 blade), 4.5 cm wide, 0.6 cm thick. 1 lb. 12 oz.

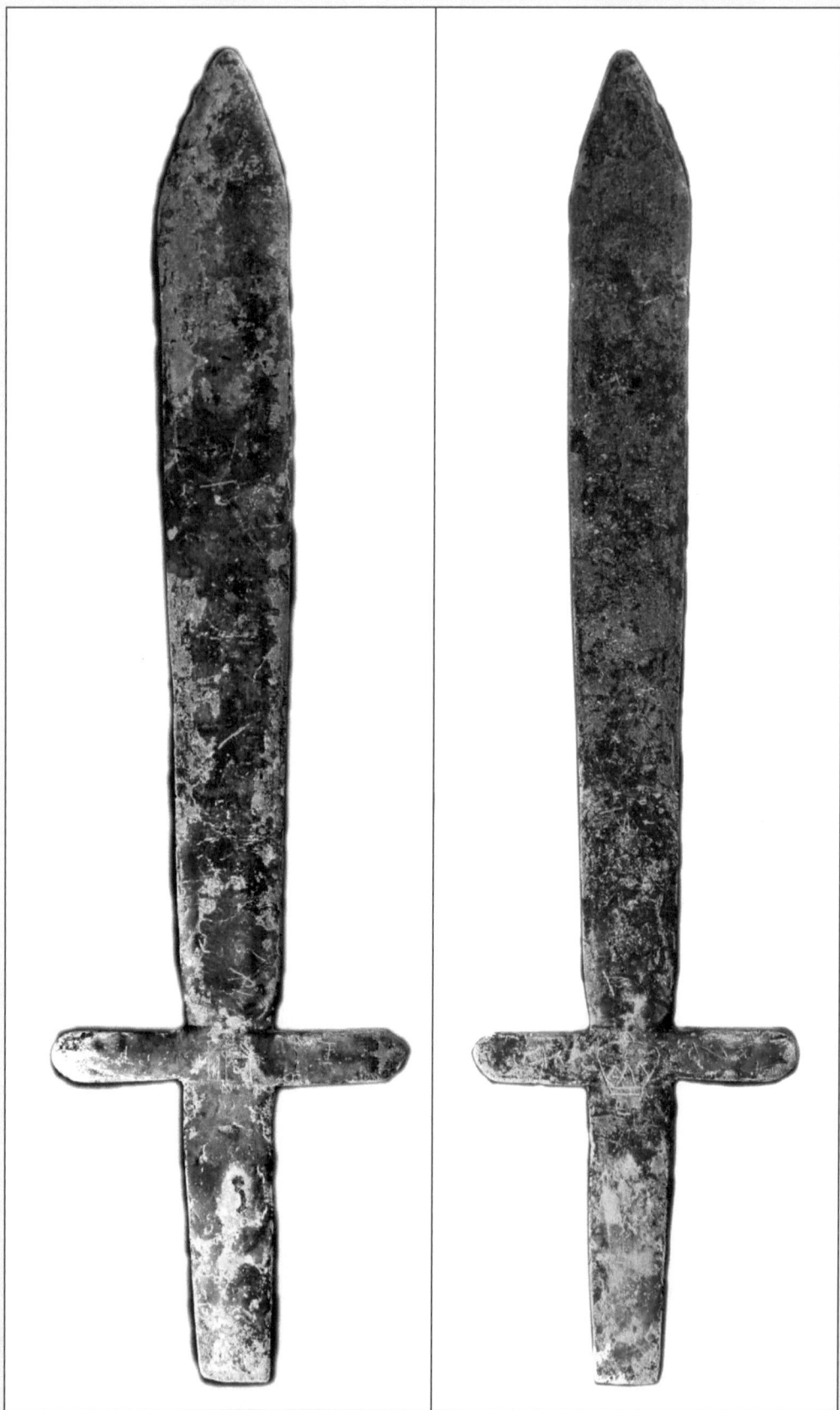

9. Javelin

Catalog #94.26.9A,B. s. IX. Hollow lead javelin broken into two pieces (A,B), haft missing. Discovered March 4, 1925 by Charles E. Manier and Thomas W. Bent, Sr. with A. E. Douglass, Thomas Lovering and C.J. Sarle. A: 21 cm long, 5.7 cm wide, 0.8 diameter. B: 25.4 cm long, 3.1 cm wide. A: 11 oz. B: 9 oz.

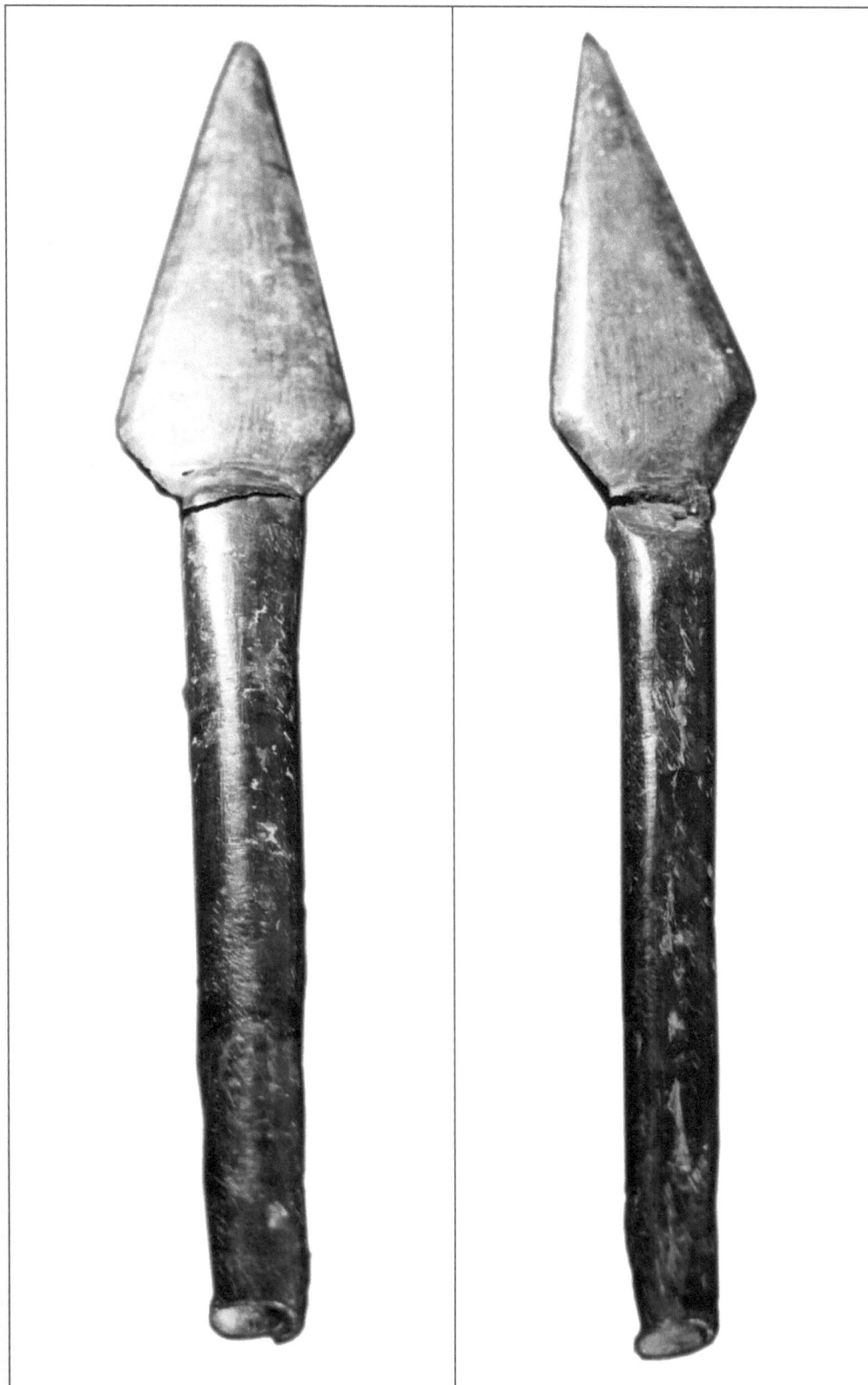

10. Spear

Catalog #94.26.10. s. IX. Solid cast lead practice or ceremonial spear or javelin, end rounded for hafting onto wood (?). Discovered March 27, 1925 by Charles E. Manier and Thomas W. Bent, Sr. with A.E. Douglass and C.J. Sarle. 25.7 cm long, shaft 27 cm long, 2.5 cm wide, 0.6 cm thick, point 20 cm long, 6 cm wide. 2 lbs. 8 oz.

11. Short Sword

Catalog #24.26.11. s. IX. Cast lead practice or ceremonial short sword (*gladius*). Discovered March 28, 1925 by A.E. Douglass with C.J. Sarle. 45.7 cm long (grip 11.4 cm), 5 cm wide (grip 4.4 cm), 0.6 cm thick. 2 lbs. 5 oz.

12. The Serpent Sword

Catalog #94.26.12. s. IX. Cast lead ceremonial or practice short sword with image of dragon or large serpent. Discovered April 4, 1925 by Charles E. Manier and Thomas W. Bent, Sr. with C.J. Sarle, Frank Fowler and Charles Vorhies. 44.5 cm long (blade 33 cm), 4.4 cm wide (grip 11.4 cm), 0.6 cm thick. 2 lbs. 15 oz.

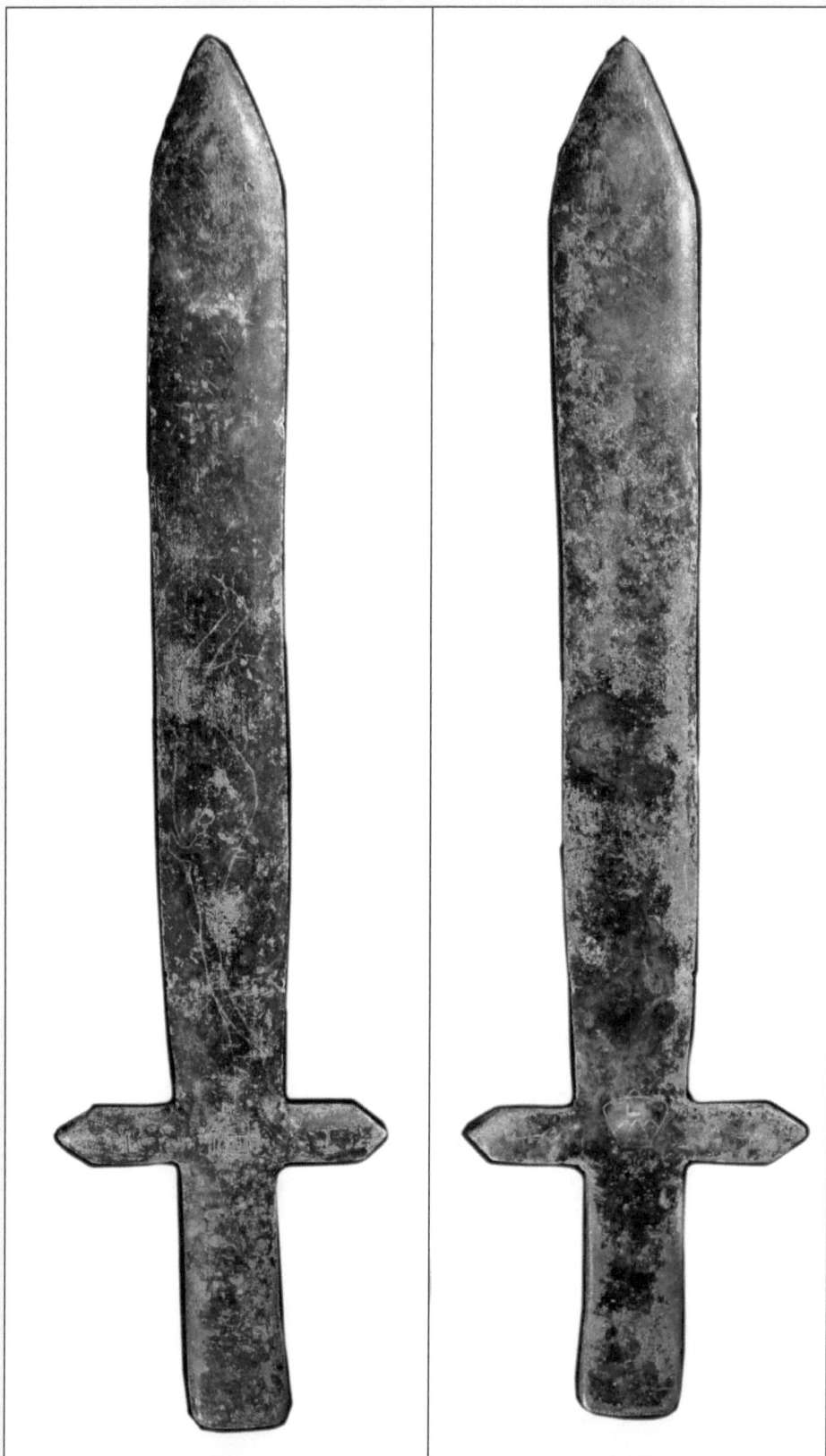

13-1. Military Standard

Catalog #94.26.13. s. IX. Fan or paddle-shaped cast lead military standard or ceremonial *labarum* with images of temples, inscriptions, markings (broken and mended). Discovered April 4, 1925 by Charles E. Manier and Thomas W. Bent, Sr. with C.J. Sarle, Frank Fowler and Charles Vorhies. 57.8 cm long (fan part 26 cm), 4.8 cm wide (fan part 22.5), 0.75 cm thick. 5 lbs. 5 oz.

L.
L. I.
Britannia
Romani
Gaule
Terra Calalus
T.
TOb
Anno Domini
DLX
(Hebrew T, N-shaped)

Levites
Levites and Israelites
Romans
Gaul
The Land of Calalus
The Land of Tob (=The Beautiful Land, Palestine)
A.D. 560
The Tau Cross (?)

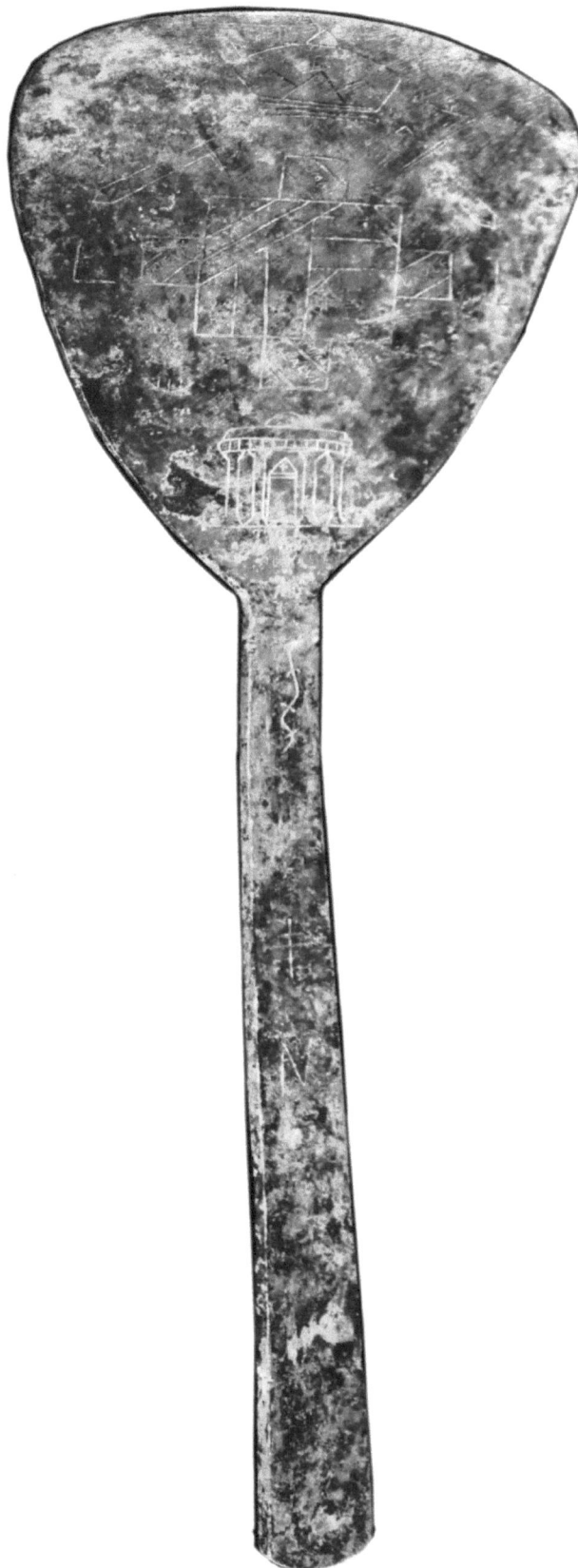

13-2. Military Standard

Catalog 94.26.12.
Reverse.

(underneath temple flanked by Frankish axes with patriarchal cross)
Tob

A.D. DCCV
L (on mitre)

The Good (Beautiful Land, Beaulande, Jerusalem) A.D. 705
Levite

14. Broken Spearhead

Catalog #94.26.14. s. IX. Cast lead broken spearhead, battered. Discovered May 26, 1925 by Charles E. Manier with A.E. Douglass, Neil Judd and C.J. Sarle. 17.8 cm long, 5.4 cm wide, 0.6 cm thick. 6 oz.

15. Broken Sword Tip

Catalog #94.26.15. s. IX. Broken tip of cast lead short sword. Discovered May 26, 1925 by Charles E. Manier with A.E. Douglass, Neil Judd and C. J. Sarle. 21 cm long, 5 cm wide, 0.6 cm thick. 15 oz.

16+23. Broken Short Sword

Catalog #94.26.16+23. s. IX. Broken upper part of cast lead ceremonial short sword going with 23, blade. Discovered July 10, 1925 by Charles E. Manier, and September 18, 1925 by unnamed worker with A.E. Douglass, Byron Cummings and C.S. Sarle. 17.8 cm long, 13.3 cm wide, 2.2 cm thick. 1 lb. 13 oz. + 28.6 cm long, 5 cm wide, 0.8 cm thick, 2 lb.

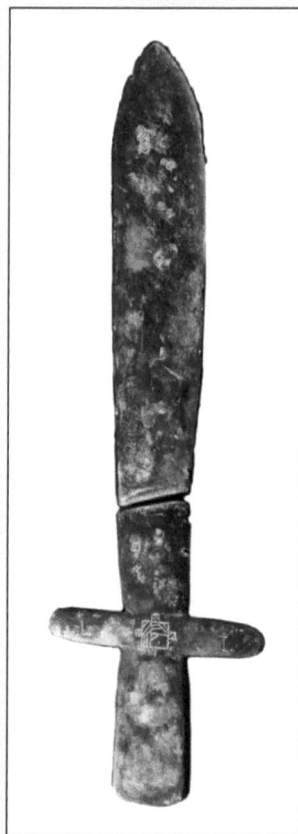

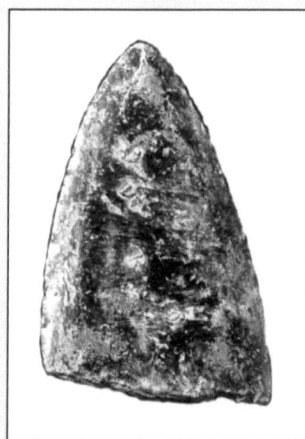

17. Sword Tip Fragment

Catalog #94.26.17. s. IX. Pointed end of cast lead ceremonial or practice sword. Discovered August 27, 1925 by Antonio Corella. 8.3 cm long, 5.6 cm wide, 0.6 cm thick. 5 oz.

18-1. Nehushtan

Catalog #94.26.18. s. IX. Cast lead *nehushtan* (ceremonial cross with serpent) inscribed in Latin and Hebrew with drawings, crest, seals and modeled snake wrapping around middle portion. Discovered August 29, 1925 by Antonio Corella. Obverse side. 44.75 cm tall, 21.5 cm wide, 0.6 cm thick. 2 lbs. 4 oz.

Hebrew inscriptions.

V-O-E
L.I.

Practice conquers all
Levites and Israelites

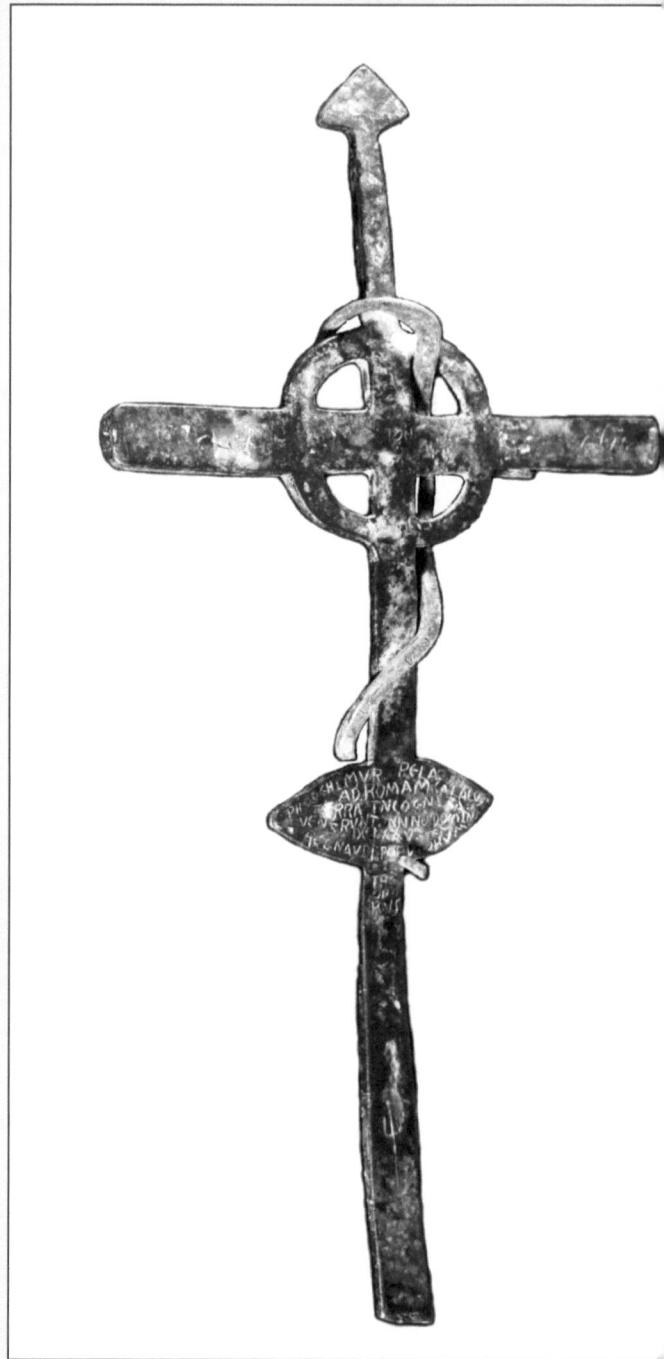

18-2 Nehushtan
Catalog #94.26.18. Reverse side.

Prouehimur pelago/ ad Romam. Calalus/ terra incognita./ Venerunt anno domini/[5] DCCLXXV et/ regnauit populorum/ The-/ odo-/ rus.

We are transports on the sea bound for Rome. Calalus was an unknown land. They came in A.D. 775 and Theodore [Natronai-Makhir, d. 793] ruled the peoples.

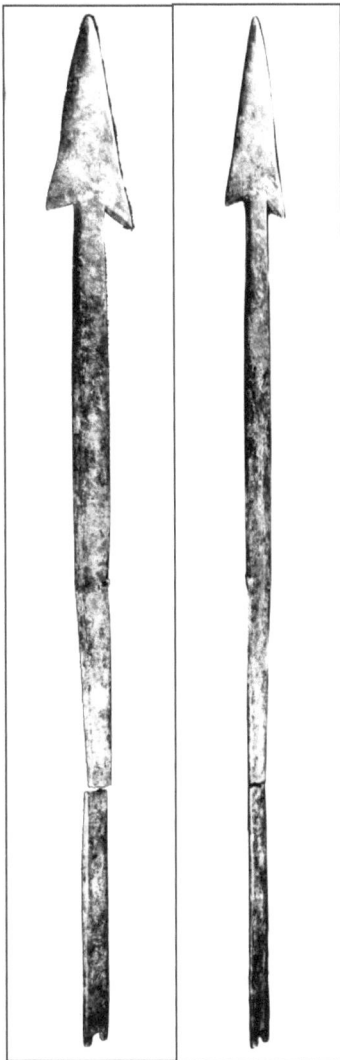

19. Broken Spear
Catalog #94.26.19. s. IX. Cast lead spear with part of shaft broken off. Goes with 21. Discovered August 30, 1925 by unnamed worker and C.J. Sarle. 55.9 cm long (spearhead 15.2 cm), 2.5 cm wide (spearhead 6 cm), 0.6 cm thick. 2 lbs. 1 oz.

21. Spear Shaft Fragment
Catalog #94.26.21. s. IX. End of lead spear shaft, hollow, notched, goes with 19. Discovered September 2, 1925 by L.A. Borquez with C.J. Sarle. 19.4 cm long, 6.7 cm wide, 0.6 cm thick. 6 oz.

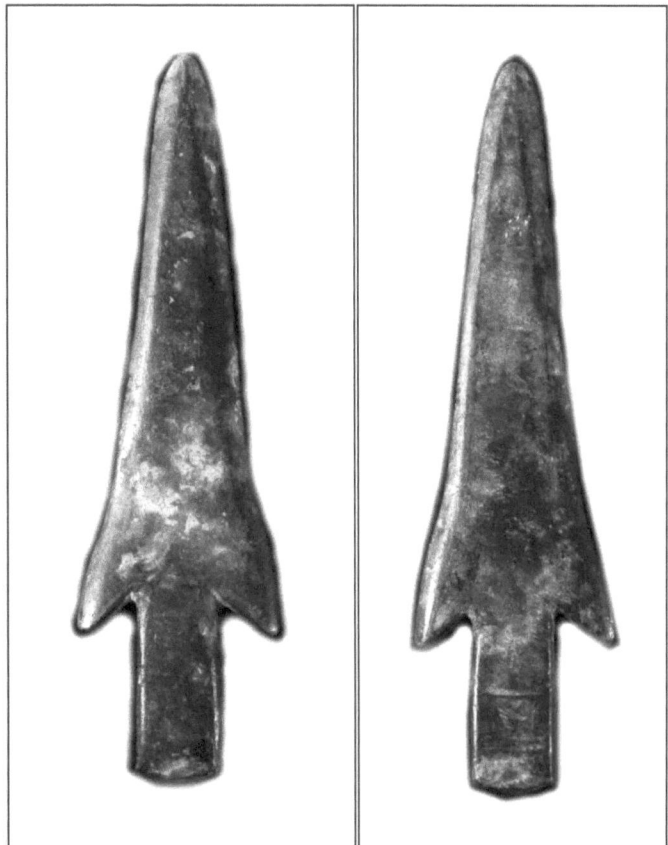

22. Spearhead
Catalog #94.26.22. s. IX. Cast lead spearhead with barbs and high copper and zinc content. Discovered September 2, 1925 by unnamed worker with A.E. Douglass, Byron Cummings and C.J. Sarle. 14.3 cm long (blade 10.8, shaft 12.75 cm), 3.3 cm wide (blade 3.8), 0.5 cm thick. 4.5 oz.

20-1. Nehushtan with Angels and Ten Commandments

Catalog #94.26.20. s. IX. Cast lead *nehushtan* or mace with crescent and cross. Discovered September 1, 1925 by unnamed worker and C.J. Sarle. 55.25 cm tall, 16 cm wide, .75 cm thick. 3 lbs. 11 oz. Obverse side.

I	VI
II	VII
III	VIII
IV	IX
V	X

Hebrew inscriptions, armed angels, angels in glory, sacrificial fire

20-2. Nehushtan
Catalog 94.26.20. Reverse side.

(beneath
thunderbird/angel/phoenix)
Sen[u]

Hebrew inscriptions.

L. I.
S.

Seven-branched candlestick.
Tang-style seal script.
Ten commandments (I-X).

24. Broken Short Sword

Catalog #94.26.24. s. IX. Cast lead ceremonial or practice sword, broken into three pieces. Discovered November 6, 1925 by Placido Ochoa. 43.8 cm long, 5-5.7 cm wide (grip 12.1 cm), 0.6 cm thick. Handle 15 oz., blade 1 lb. 10 oz., end of handle. 6 oz. 2 lbs. 15 oz. altogether.

25+28. Broken Spearhead

Catalog #94.26.25+28. s. IX. Head of lead spear in two pieces, goes with 30. Discovered November 6, 1925 by Ricardo Balancuela. 5.1 cm long, 1.9 cm wide, 0.6 cm thick. 9 oz. Discovered February 11, 1928 by E. John Hand of the University of Arizona Excavation Team under Byron Cummings. 14 cm long, 4.4 cm wide, 0.6 cm thick. 7 oz.

26. Short Sword

Catalog #94.26.26. s. IX. Cast lead inscribed ceremonial or practice sword; compare to 16/23. Discovered November 7, 1925 by unnamed worker and John S. Bent. 44 cm long (blade 33 long), 5.8 cm wide (grip 12.1 cm), 0.5 cm thick. 2 lbs. 8 oz.

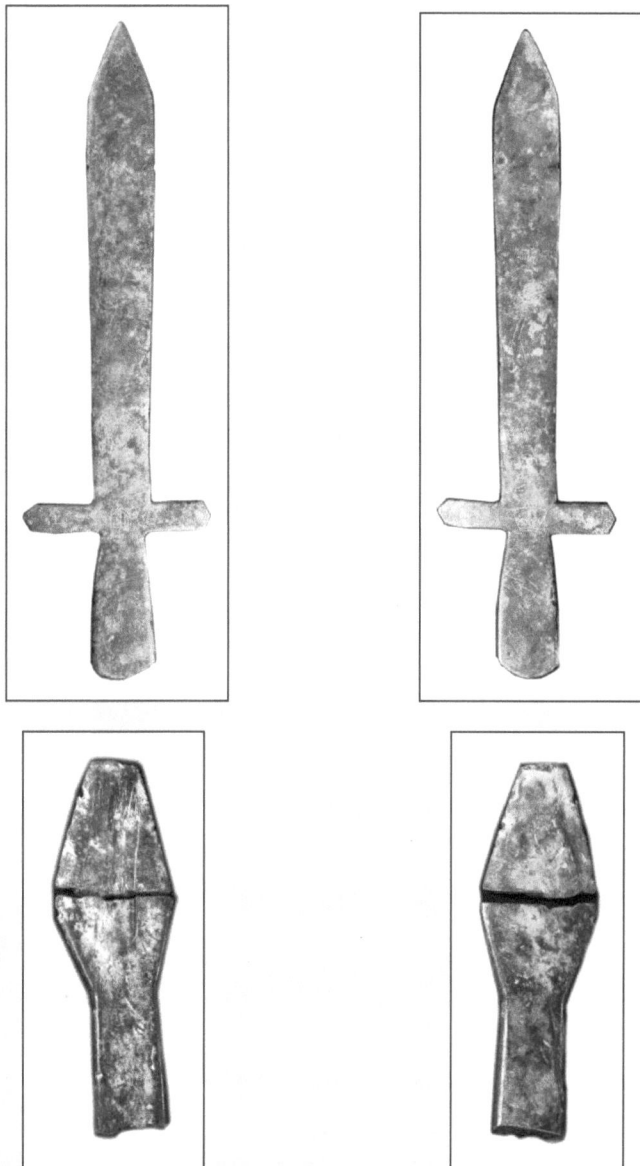

27. Spearhead Fragment

Catalog #94.26.27. s. IX. Cast lead spearhead missing tip, goes with 29. Discovered November 13, 1925 by John S. Bent. 4.5 cm long, 3.7 cm wide, 0.5 cm thick. 1.6 oz.

29. Spear Fragment

Catalog #94.26.29. s. IX. Part of spearhead and shaft of cast lead spear, goes with 27. Discovered February 9, 1928 by E. John Hand of the University of Arizona Excavation Team under Byron Cummings. 7.3 cm long, 3.8 cm wide, 0.6 cm thick. 3.1 oz.

30. Spear Fragments

Catalog #94.26.30. s. IX. Two pieces of cast lead spear shaft, going with 25 and 28. Discovered February 11, 1928 by Gurdon Montague Butler of the University of Arizona Excavation Team under Byron Cummings. First piece: 4.4 cm long, 2.5 cm wide, 0.6 cm thick. Second piece: 16.5 cm cm long, 2.5 cm wide, 0.6 cm thick. 8 oz., 1.5 oz.

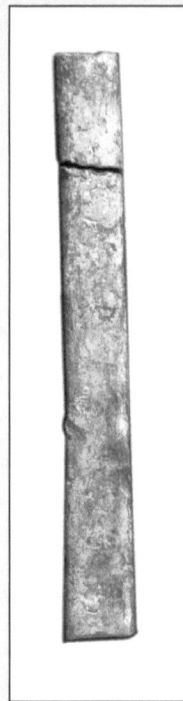

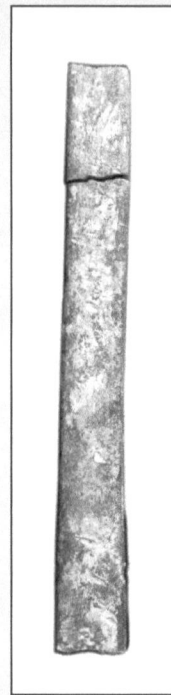

31. Broken Spear

Catalog 94.26.31. s. IX. Cast lead spear or javelin, point broken, shaft at bottom broken, barbed. Discovered March 3, 1928. By Charles B. Conrad of the University of Arizona Excavation Team under Byron Cummings. Overall length 31.75 (blade 4.4 cm, shaft 24.8 cm), 2.5-7 cm wide, 0.5-0.6 cm thick. 12 oz.

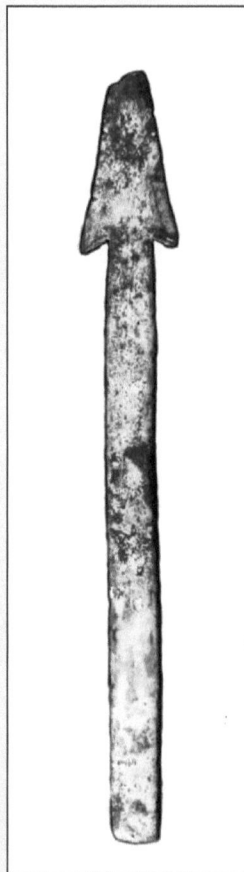

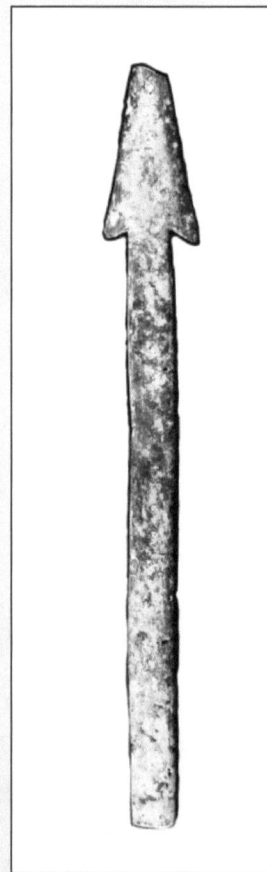

32. Spear Shaft Fragment

Catalog #94.26.32. s. IX. Part of shaft of cast lead practice or ceremonial spear. Discovered March 15, 1930 by John S. Bent. 22.9 cm long, 1.9 cm wide, 0.6 cm thick. 9 oz.

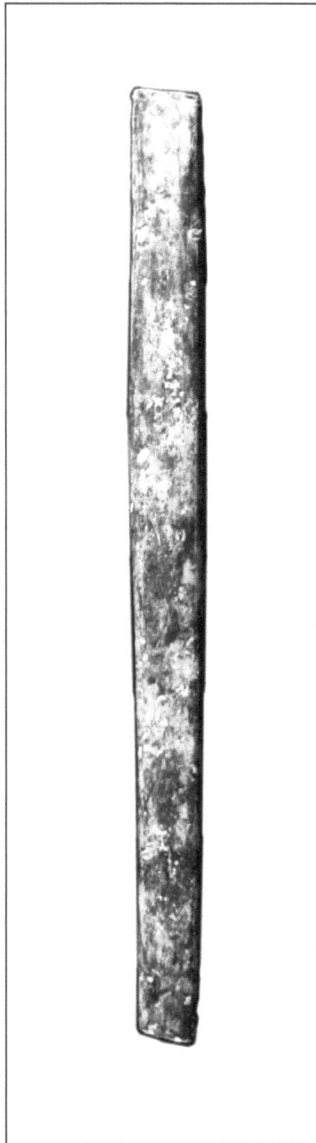

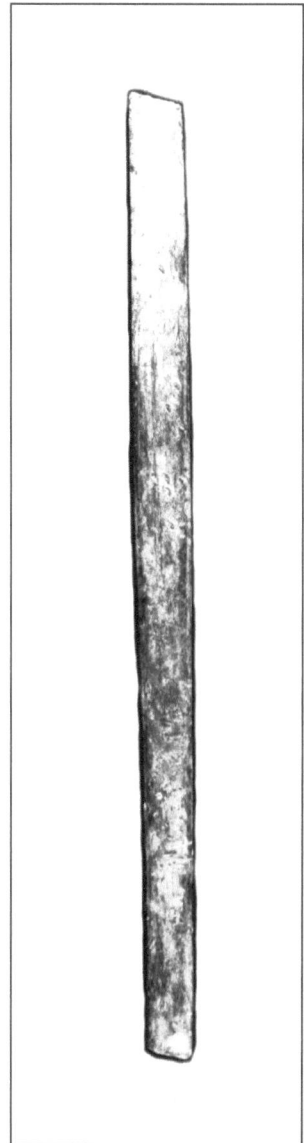

This book was set in Book Antiqua, a letterform modeled on
Roman inscriptional capitals and Carolingian writing.
It was pioneered by the French engraver Nicolas
Jenson (1404-1480) and prized for its beauty
and perfection by the English Arts
and Crafts designer William
Morris (1834-1896).

www.ingramcontent.com/pod-product-compliance
Lightning Source LLC
Chambersburg PA
CBHW042007080426
42733CB00003B/32